ANTALYA

TRAVEL GUIDE 2024-2025

Mediterranean Marvels: Explore Beaches, Historical Sites, and Hidden Gems for the Ultimate Turkish Escape

PAUL R. BAKER

TABLE OF CONTENTS

SCAN THE QR CODE TO ACCESS THE ANTALYA MAP

INTRODUCTION TO ANTALYA

Antalya, a jewel of Turkey's Turquoise Coast, is poised to offer a remarkable travel experience in 2024-2025. With its blend of stunning Mediterranean coastline and richly woven history, the city is more than just a scenic escape—it's a vibrant, living museum where every stone tells a story. Recent developments have only enhanced its allure.

The completion of the new cultural complex in the Kaleiçi district offers visitors a deep dive into the arts and heritage of the region, while the annual Antalya Film Festival continues to attract cinema enthusiasts from across the globe. What's more, the city is fast becoming a hub for eco-tourism, inviting travelers to explore its lush landscapes and pristine beaches responsibly.

My journey to Antalya was nothing short of magical. As I strolled through the winding streets of Kaleiçi, the historic heart of the city, I was enveloped by a sense of community that's palpable at every corner. It's a town where traditions are alive, passed down through families who have rooted their lives here for generations. The local bazaars brimmed with artisans showcasing their crafts, each piece a reflection of Antalya's artistic spirit. I was particularly drawn to the landscape—rugged mountains sweeping down to meet the sea, offering breathtaking vistas that promised endless adventures.

You will find that Antalya's past is as colorful as the bougainvillea that adorns its old stone walls. This city, once a major Roman port, has seen empires rise and fall, each leaving behind remnants that make up the rich tapestry of its history. Notable sites include Hadrian's Gate, built to honor the Roman emperor's visit in 130 AD, and the ancient city of Aspendos, boasting one of the best-preserved Roman theatres in the world.

Antalya's commitment to preserving these treasures while embracing modernity makes it a unique destination for those who seek a deeper understanding of the places they visit.

In my exploration, I discovered the distinct flavors of Antalya's five towns, each with its own character. Alanya, with its famed Red Tower and bustling markets, offers a glimpse into the region's Seljuk heritage. Kemer lures nature lovers with its pine-fringed beaches and the nearby Olympos Beydağları National Park. Belek, a paradise for golf enthusiasts, boasts world-class courses alongside luxurious resorts. Side charms with its blend of sandy beaches and Greco-Roman ruins, while Kas, a haven for divers, reveals underwater wonders and a laid-back bohemian vibe.

As my journey drew to a close, I realized that leaving Antalya was not goodbye, but a promise to return. The city, with its endless stories and welcoming locals, stays with you long after you depart. Whether you're seeking adventure, tranquility, or cultural enrichment, Antalya offers it all and then some. So pack your bags and set your sights on this Mediterranean marvel—you won't want to miss what Antalya has in store for you in the coming years.

Historical Significance and Cultural Richness

Antalya's history dates back to the second century BCE when it was founded by King Attalus II of Pergamon, who named it Attaleia after himself. Throughout its history, Antalya has been a significant hub for various civilizations, including the Romans, Byzantines, Seljuks, and Ottomans. Each of these cultures has left an indelible mark on the city, evident in its architectural marvels and historical landmarks. The ancient city of Perge, with its well-preserved ruins, and the Aspendos Theatre, one of the best-preserved ancient theaters in the world, are testaments to Antalya's rich historical heritage.

Ancient Beginnings

The history of Antalya stretches back to antiquity. Originally known as Attaleia, the city was founded in 150 BC by the Pergamene King Attalus II. The name "Attaleia" was a tribute to its founder, and the city was strategically located on the Mediterranean coast, making it an essential hub for trade and military activity. Under Roman rule, Antalya flourished as a vital port city, its prosperity bolstered by its advantageous location on the ancient trade routes connecting Europe and Asia.

Roman and Byzantine Eras

During the Roman Empire, Antalya expanded significantly, with many of its ancient structures dating from this period.

The city became an important administrative and economic center, evidenced by the grand Hadrian's Gate, constructed in honor of Emperor Hadrian's visit in 130 AD. The gate remains one of the most iconic symbols of Roman influence in Antalya.

As the Roman Empire transitioned into the Byzantine Empire, Antalya continued to thrive. The Byzantines reinforced the city's defensive walls and constructed religious buildings, contributing to the city's rich architectural heritage. The transformation of Attaleia into Antalya also marked the beginning of a new era, with the city becoming a melting pot of cultural influences.

Seljuk and Ottoman Periods

The Seljuk Turks arrived in Antalya in the late 11th century, significantly impacting the city's cultural and architectural landscape. The Seljuks left a lasting legacy, including the construction of the Yivli Minaret Mosque and several other Islamic buildings that exemplify the Seljuk architectural style. This period saw the integration of Islamic art and culture into Antalya's already diverse heritage.

The Ottoman Empire, which began its dominance in the late 14th century, further enriched Antalya's cultural fabric. The Ottomans brought stability and prosperity to the city, turning it into a significant administrative center.

This era saw the construction of various Ottoman-era structures, including caravanserais and bathhouses, that served both locals and travelers.

Modern Era and Cultural Synthesis

In the 20th century, Antalya underwent rapid modernization, transitioning from a sleepy town into a bustling city. The establishment of the Republic of Turkey in 1923 marked a new phase in Antalya's history, as it adapted to the modern state while preserving its historical and cultural roots. The city's tourism boom in recent decades has introduced a new dimension to its cultural identity, blending historical charm with contemporary amenities.

Today, Antalya stands as a testament to the rich tapestry of its past. The city's diverse heritage is evident in its architecture, ranging from ancient Roman ruins to Seljuk mosques and Ottoman buildings. Cultural festivals, traditional arts, and culinary traditions reflect the city's historical layers, showcasing a blend of Greek, Roman, Byzantine, Seljuk, and Ottoman influences.

Shaping Today's Identity

Antalya's identity today is a reflection of its historical evolution. The city's unique position at the crossroads of cultures has fostered a rich cultural synthesis that continues to shape its character. The preservation of historical sites alongside modern developments offers visitors a glimpse into the city's layered past, while its vibrant cultural scene and dynamic tourism industry ensure that Antalya remains a thriving and welcoming destination.

Geographical Features

Antalya is cradled by the Taurus Mountains to the north, which rise dramatically from the coastal plain, creating a stunning backdrop to the city's turquoise Mediterranean shoreline. These mountains, with their rugged peaks and verdant slopes, are interspersed with fertile valleys and deep canyons, enhancing the region's natural beauty. To the south, the Mediterranean coast is dotted with a mix of rocky cliffs and sandy beaches, offering diverse waterfront experiences. The city itself is perched on a picturesque bay, providing panoramic views of the sea that blend seamlessly with the ancient architecture of the old town,

Climatic Conditions

The climate in Antalya is characterized by a typical Mediterranean pattern, marked by hot, dry summers and mild, wet winters. From May to October, visitors can expect long, sun-drenched days with temperatures often exceeding 30°C (86°F). This period is ideal for beach activities, boating, and outdoor exploration. The sun-drenched beaches and warm sea temperatures make summer a peak season for tourists seeking sun and sea.

In contrast, the winter months, from November to April, are much cooler and more temperate, with daytime temperatures ranging from 10°C to 20°C (50°F to 68°F).

Although rain is more frequent during this season, the climate remains relatively mild compared to many other destinations, making it suitable for exploring the region’s cultural and historical sites without the intensity of summer heat.

Impact on Travel Experiences: Antalya's diverse geography and climate profoundly influence travel activities and experiences. The summer’s warmth and dry weather make it perfect for beachgoers and outdoor enthusiasts. Activities such as snorkeling, diving, and paragliding are best enjoyed during this time when the sea is calm and the skies are clear. The favorable weather conditions also support a thriving outdoor cafe culture and numerous festivals that take advantage of the sunny days.

During the cooler winter months, the mild temperatures and reduced crowds offer a different appeal. This is an excellent time for cultural tourism, with fewer tourists and more comfortable conditions for visiting historical sites like Hadrian's Gate and the ancient city of Perge. The winter rains, while infrequent, enhance the lushness of the landscapes and rejuvenate the waterfalls and natural springs, providing scenic beauty that contrasts with the dry summer.

Unique Aspects of Antalya

Several unique aspects make Antalya stand out as a premier travel destination. The city is a gateway to the Lycian Way, one of the world's top long-distance hiking trails, offering breathtaking coastal views and ancient ruins. Antalya is also famous for its Blue Flag beaches, which meet high environmental and quality standards, ensuring clean and safe swimming conditions.

Moreover, Antalya's culinary scene is a delightful exploration of Turkish cuisine, with a focus on fresh, locally sourced ingredients. From traditional kebabs and mezes to seafood caught daily from the Mediterranean, the city's dining options cater to all tastes.

PLANNING YOUR TRIP

When to Visit

Spring (March to May)

- **Weather Patterns**: Spring in Antalya is characterized by mild temperatures, ranging from 15°C to 25°C (59°F to 77°F). The weather is pleasantly warm and the landscapes are lush and blooming, making it ideal for sightseeing and outdoor activities.

- **Seasonal Highlights**: This is the perfect time for exploring Antalya's historical sites and natural wonders without the summer crowds. The blooming flowers and greenery enhance the beauty of gardens and parks.
- **Special Events**:
    - **Antalya International Film Festival (April)**: Celebrates global cinema with screenings, workshops, and guest appearances from industry professionals.
    - **Antalya Piano Festival (May)**: Features performances by international and Turkish pianists, offering a cultural treat for music lovers.
- **Travel Tips**: Early spring is ideal for hiking and exploring ancient ruins, as the temperatures are comfortable and the terrain is not too hot. Booking accommodations in advance is recommended as festivals can attract more visitors.

Summer (June to August)

- **Weather Patterns**: Antalya experiences hot and dry weather during summer, with temperatures soaring between 25°C and 35°C (77°F to 95°F).

The sun is strong, making this a peak season for beach-goers and sunbathers.

- **Seasonal Highlights**: The summer months are perfect for enjoying Antalya's beautiful beaches, such as Lara and Konyaaltı, as well as indulging in water sports and boat trips. The clear blue skies and warm sea temperatures create an ideal environment for outdoor activities.
- **Special Events**:
  - **Antalya Sand Sculpture Festival (June - September)**: Held at Lara Beach, this festival features impressive sand sculptures created by artists from around the world.
  - **Aspendos International Opera and Ballet Festival (June - July)**: A prestigious event held in the ancient Aspendos Theatre, offering a unique experience of opera and ballet in a historic setting.
- **Travel Tips**: It's advisable to stay hydrated, use sunscreen, and seek shade during the hottest parts of the day. Early bookings for accommodations and tours are crucial, as this is the high season for tourism.

Autumn (September to November)

- **Weather Patterns**: Autumn brings cooler temperatures, ranging from 20°C to 30°C (68°F to 86°F), and the weather is generally pleasant with less humidity. The sea remains warm enough for swimming well into October.
- **Seasonal Highlights**: The cooler weather makes this season ideal for exploring Antalya's cultural and historical sites, as well as enjoying outdoor activities such as hiking in the nearby Taurus Mountains.
- **Special Events**:
  - **Antalya Golden Orange Film Festival (October)**: A major film festival celebrating Turkish cinema with screenings, awards, and industry networking.
  - **Harvest Festivals (October - November)**: Various local festivals celebrating the harvest season with traditional music, food, and folk dances.
- **Travel Tips**: Autumn is a great time to visit for those who prefer fewer crowds and more moderate temperatures. It's also a good period for taking scenic drives and enjoying local festivities.

Winter (December to February)

- **Weather Patterns**: Winter in Antalya is mild compared to other Turkish cities, with temperatures averaging between 10°C and 20°C (50°F to 68°F). While it's cooler and wetter, it's still relatively mild compared to much of Europe.
- **Seasonal Highlights**: Winter is ideal for those looking to explore Antalya's historic sites and cultural attractions without the heat of summer. It's also a good time for enjoying a quieter experience and taking advantage of off-season prices.
- **Special Events**:
  - **New Year Celebrations (December 31)**: The city comes alive with festivities, including fireworks and special events at hotels and restaurants.
  - **Antalya Museum's Winter Exhibitions**: Various temporary exhibitions are hosted during the winter months, providing a cultural insight into the region's history and art.
- **Travel Tips**: Pack layers to adjust to varying temperatures and expect some rainfall.

It’s a good time to explore indoor attractions and enjoy local cuisine in a more relaxed atmosphere.

Unique Insights for Travelers

- **Weather Preparedness**: Be aware of the significant temperature variations between seasons and pack accordingly. Summers require sun protection and hydration, while winters necessitate warmer clothing and rain gear.
- **Local Festivals**: Attending local festivals not only enriches your travel experience but also offers insight into the region’s culture and traditions. These events can be great opportunities for social interaction and cultural immersion.
- **Crowds and Costs**: Traveling during shoulder seasons (spring and autumn) can offer a balanced experience with fewer crowds and more moderate prices, while summer offers vibrant beach activities and festivals but requires early bookings due to high demand.

How to Get There

International Flights

Antalya is well-connected to major cities across Europe and beyond through its international airport, Antalya Airport (AYT). Direct flights are available from numerous European cities, including Berlin, London, Paris, and Amsterdam. Here's how to make your international journey as smooth as possible:

- **Book Early**: Secure your flights well in advance to get the best rates and availability.
- **Check for Direct Routes**: Opt for direct flights to save time and avoid layovers.
- **Arrive Early**: Arrive at the airport with plenty of time to navigate security and check-in.

2. Domestic Flights

For travelers coming from within Turkey, Antalya Airport is also a major hub. Frequent flights are available from cities such as Istanbul, Ankara, and Izmir. Tips for domestic travelers include:

- **Use Budget Airlines**: Turkish domestic flights are often serviced by budget airlines like Pegasus and AnadoluJet, which can offer cost-effective options.

- **Consider Flight Times**: Early morning or late evening flights can be less crowded and more affordable.

3. Bus Services

Antalya is accessible by bus from various parts of Turkey. Major bus companies operate services connecting Antalya with cities like Istanbul, Ankara, and İzmir.

- **Book in Advance**: Ensure your seat by booking tickets online or at bus terminals ahead of time.
- **Choose a Comfortable Service**: Opt for a luxury bus service with amenities such as Wi-Fi and refreshments for a more comfortable journey.
- **Check Arrival Points**: Be aware that some buses might arrive at different terminals, so confirm your drop-off point.

4. Train Services

While Antalya itself is not directly connected to the national rail network, you can take a train to a nearby city such as Isparta or Burdur and then continue by bus or car.

- **Combine Modes of Transport**: Plan a combined train and bus journey for a scenic and relaxing trip.

- **Check Schedules**: Verify train and bus schedules to ensure smooth connections.

5. Road Travel

Driving to Antalya is a great option for those who enjoy road trips. The city is accessible via well-maintained highways from major cities across Turkey.

- **Rent a Car**: If you're not driving your own vehicle, consider renting a car for flexibility and convenience.
- **Plan Your Route**: Use GPS or a navigation app to plan your route and check for any roadworks or detours.
- **Check Road Conditions**: Be aware of road conditions, especially in mountainous areas, and ensure your vehicle is in good condition.

Unique Tips for a Smooth Journey

- **Travel Insurance**: Always travel with insurance to cover any unexpected issues during your journey.
- **Local Transport Apps**: Download apps for local transportation and navigation to ease your travel around Antalya.
- **Pack Essentials**: Carry essentials like snacks, water, and travel documents in an easily accessible part of your bag.

- **Stay Informed**: Keep up with any travel advisories or updates regarding your chosen mode of transport.

Transportation in Antalya

Public Transport

Antalya's public transportation system is efficient and well-connected, making it easy to navigate the city.

- **Buses:** The city's bus network, managed by the Antalya Metropolitan Municipality, covers most areas including tourist spots, residential neighborhoods, and business districts. Buses are a cost-effective way to get around, with routes clearly marked and schedules generally reliable. For travelers, the use of an AntalyaKart is recommended, which can be purchased at kiosks or vending machines around the city and loaded with credit for seamless travel on buses and trams.
- **Trams:** Antalya's tram system, known as the **AntRay**, primarily serves the central and southern parts of the city, connecting key locations like the airport, the Old Town (Kaleiçi), and the port area. Trams are a comfortable option, offering frequent services with clean and air-conditioned cars.

2. Taxis

- **Standard Taxis:** Easily identifiable by their yellow color, taxis in Antalya are plentiful and can be hailed from the street, found at taxi stands, or booked via phone or mobile apps. They are generally reliable and offer a door-to-door service. Ensure that the meter is running to avoid disputes over fares.
- **Airport Transfers:** For convenience, especially when arriving or departing, consider booking an airport transfer service. Many companies offer pre-arranged transfers that provide a fixed fare and eliminate the stress of navigating taxis or public transport with luggage.

3. Car Rentals

- **Renting a Car:** Renting a car is a great option if you plan to explore beyond Antalya or if you prefer the flexibility of self-driving. The city hosts a variety of rental agencies, each providing an assortment of vehicles. Car rentals provide the freedom to visit nearby attractions like the ancient city of Perge or the beautiful beaches around the coast. However, parking in central Antalya can be challenging, so be sure to check for available parking facilities or opt for accommodations with dedicated parking.

- **Driving Tips:** Be aware that traffic can be heavy during peak hours, and local driving habits might be different from what you're used to. Make use of GPS navigation systems to avoid getting lost and to find the quickest routes.

4. Biking

- **Cycling:** Antalya is increasingly becoming bike-friendly, with several dedicated bike lanes and scenic routes along the coast. Renting a bike can be a pleasant way to explore the city, especially along the picturesque Konyaaltı Beach promenade or through the charming streets of Kaleiçi. Several rental shops offer bikes for short or long-term hire, and some accommodations may provide bike rentals as well.

Unique Advice for Navigating Antalya Efficiently:

- **Plan Ahead:** Check public transport schedules and routes before setting out. Apps like **Antalya Transit** provide real-time updates and route planning to make your journey smoother.

- **Stay Central:** If you're staying in or near Kaleiçi, most attractions are within walking distance, reducing the need for transport. The narrow, winding streets are best explored on foot.
- **Use Ride-Sharing Apps:** Apps like **Uber** and **BiTaksi** are operational in Antalya and can be more convenient than traditional taxis, offering transparent pricing and the ability to track your ride.
- **Explore on Two Wheels:** For short distances and a bit of local flavor, consider renting an e-bike or a traditional bicycle. It's an eco-friendly way to experience the city at your own pace and discover hidden gems.

Visa and Entry Requirements

1. Visa Requirements

a. Short-Term Tourist Visas:

- **Schengen Visa:** Antalya, as part of Turkey, does not fall under the Schengen Area. However, many travelers from the Schengen Area can enter Turkey visa-free for up to 90 days within a 180-day period.
- **E-Visa:** Travelers from eligible countries can apply for a Turkish e-Visa online.

The e-Visa allows for short stays up to 90 days and is an efficient option for many tourists. It is essential to apply at least 48 hours before departure.

b. Visa on Arrival:

- **Not Available:** Turkey has largely phased out visa-on-arrival options. Travelers must secure their visa beforehand through e-Visa or the Turkish embassy/consulate in their country.

c. Special Cases:

- **Long-Term Stays:** For stays exceeding 90 days, travelers must apply for a residence permit or a long-term visa at a Turkish embassy or consulate before traveling.

2. Recent Changes and Updates

- **Updated E-Visa System:** The e-Visa system now includes new security measures and an extended list of eligible countries. Always check the official Turkish e-Visa website for the most current eligibility and application requirements.
- **COVID-19 Regulations:** As of 2024, Turkey has relaxed many COVID-19 restrictions. However, travelers should confirm if any health declarations or

proof of vaccination are required closer to their travel date.

- **Biometric Data:** New regulations require biometric data (photo and fingerprints) at entry points for certain visa types, enhancing border security and processing efficiency.

3. Tips for a Hassle-Free Entry Process

a. Double-Check Visa Validity:

- Ensure that your visa is valid for the entire duration of your stay. Verify that all information on your visa is correct and matches your passport details.

b. Apply Early:

- Apply for your e-Visa or other required documents well in advance to avoid last-minute issues. Allow at least two weeks before your departure to account for any unforeseen delays.

c. Keep Documents Handy:

- Have a printed copy of your e-Visa, passport, and any supporting documents (such as hotel reservations or return tickets) readily accessible. This can expedite the entry process.

[illegible]

[illegible]

[illegible]

[illegible]

[illegible]

[illegible]

d. Follow Entry Procedures:

- Familiarize yourself with the standard entry procedures at Antalya Airport. Be prepared for biometric scans if required, and follow instructions from border control officers.

e. Travel Insurance:

- Consider purchasing travel insurance that covers visa issues and medical emergencies. This can provide peace of mind and additional support in case of any unexpected problems.

f. Stay Informed:

- Stay updated on any travel advisories or changes in entry requirements through official Turkish government sources or your country's embassy in Turkey.

g. Contact Information:

- Save contact details for the nearest Turkish consulate or embassy in case you encounter issues with your visa or entry. They can provide assistance and guidance.

TOP ATTRACTIONS IN ANTALYA

Old Town (Kaleiçi)

Historical Context: Kaleiçi is the historic heart of Antalya, boasting a rich tapestry of history that dates back to Roman times. The area was originally founded as a port city, and its architecture reflects a blend of Roman, Byzantine, Seljuk, and Ottoman influences. Kaleiçi was enclosed by city walls that still stand today, offering a glimpse into its ancient past.

Unique Features: Wander through the narrow, winding streets of Kaleiçi, and you'll encounter charming Ottoman-era houses with their characteristic wooden balconies and intricate carvings.

Key landmarks include the Yivli Minare Mosque, a striking 13th-century Seljuk structure with a distinctive fluted minaret, and the Clock Tower, which marks the entrance to the old town. The area also features picturesque courtyards and artisan shops selling local crafts and souvenirs.

Practical Visiting Tips:

- Wear comfortable walking shoes, as the streets can be uneven.
- Visit the old town early in the day to avoid crowds and enjoy a more peaceful experience.
- Many restaurants and cafes in Kaleiçi offer beautiful views and traditional Turkish cuisine, making it an ideal spot for a meal.

Hadrian's Gate

Historical Context: Hadrian's Gate, also known as Üçkapılar, was constructed in 130 AD to honor the Roman Emperor Hadrian's visit to the city. This triumphal arch is a testament to the grandeur of Roman architecture and serves as one of the best-preserved ancient monuments in Antalya.

Unique Features: The gate is notable for its ornate marble decorations and intricate reliefs depicting mythological scenes. Its three arched openings are flanked by towers, which were once part of the city's fortifications. The structure's grandeur is further highlighted by its impressive Corinthian columns and the beautifully carved friezes that adorn its surfaces.

Practical Visiting Tips:

- The gate is located near Kaleiçi, so it can easily be combined with a visit to the old town.

- Early morning or late afternoon visits can provide better lighting for photographs and a quieter experience.
- The area around the gate is pedestrian-friendly, making it easy to explore on foot.

Aspendos Theatre

Historical Context: Aspendos Theatre is one of the best-preserved ancient theatres in the world, dating back to the 2nd century AD. It was built during the Roman period under

Emperor Marcus Aurelius and could seat up to 15,000 spectators.

The theatre is renowned for its remarkable acoustics and architectural design.

Unique Features: The theatre's semi-circular auditorium is complemented by a well-preserved stage building with intricate reliefs and decorative elements. The acoustics are so precise that even a whisper on stage can be heard clearly throughout the seating area. The site also offers stunning views of the surrounding countryside and provides insight into ancient Roman entertainment and culture.

Practical Visiting Tips:

- Attend one of the performances held at the theatre during the summer months to experience its exceptional acoustics firsthand.
- Wear a hat and sunscreen, as the site can get very hot, especially during midday.
- Bring water and wear comfortable clothing, as there is limited shade and the site involves a fair amount of walking.

Kekova and Demre

Kekova:

Kekova is a beautiful island in the Mediterranean Sea, renowned for its scenic views and historical significance. Located just off the coast of Demre, it provides a unique combination of natural beauty and ancient history.

- **Historical Significance**: Kekova is known for its submerged ruins, which are remnants of the ancient Lycian city of Dolichiste.

The city was partially destroyed by an earthquake in the 2nd century AD, and today, parts of the city, including streets, houses, and a bathhouse, are visible through the clear waters.

- **Boat Tours**: The best way to explore Kekova is by boat. Tours typically depart from the nearby towns of Üçağız or Demre, offering stunning views of the island's coastline and the submerged ruins. Boat tours often include stops at various points of interest such as the Sunken City, Kekova Village, and Simena Castle. For a more relaxed experience, opt for tours in the early morning or late afternoon to avoid peak tourist times.
- **Unique Experiences**: Visit the fortress of Simena, which provides a panoramic view of the surrounding area. The fortress is accessible via a short, moderately challenging hike and offers a unique vantage point over the submerged ruins and nearby islands.
- **Practical Tips**: Bring sunscreen, a hat, and plenty of water, as the weather can be quite hot during the summer months. If you plan to swim or explore the beaches around Kekova, wear swimwear. Many boat tours provide snorkeling equipment, so check in advance if you wish to explore the underwater ruins.

Demre:

Demre, historically known as Myra, is a region rich in historical and cultural significance, featuring a range of ancient sites and landmarks.

- **Ancient Myra**: Explore the ancient city of Myra, famous for its rock-cut tombs carved into the cliffs. These tombs, dating back to the 4th century BC, showcase Lycian burial practices and architectural style. The well-preserved Roman theater, with its stage and seating, adds to the city's historical allure.

- **Church of St. Nicholas**: Visit the Church of St. Nicholas, an important Christian site and believed to be the original resting place of St. Nicholas, the figure who inspired the legend of Santa Claus. The 6th-century church features beautiful frescoes and mosaics. If possible, attend a service or special event to experience local traditions and the church's cultural significance.

- **Local Culture and Markets**: Explore the local markets in Demre to experience traditional Turkish culture. The markets offer fresh produce, local crafts, and traditional foods. Sampling local delicacies and interacting with vendors provides a deeper understanding of the region's culture.

- **Practical Tips**: Wear comfortable walking shoes as you will be exploring historical sites with uneven terrain. Make sure to bring a hat and water, particularly in the warmer months. Arrive early at the Church of St. Nicholas to avoid crowds and have ample time to appreciate the site.

Travel Tips for Kekova and Demre:

- **Getting There**: To reach Kekova and Demre from Antalya, you can take a bus or drive, which takes approximately 1.5 to 2 hours.

Alternatively, guided tours often include transportation, offering a convenient option for a structured visit.

- **Guided Tours**: Consider booking a guided tour that covers both Kekova and Demre for a more comprehensive experience. Guides can provide historical context, answer questions, and help you navigate the sites effectively.

- **Accommodation**: For a more immersive experience, stay in local guesthouses or small hotels in Demre. This allows for a more leisurely exploration and an opportunity to enjoy local hospitality.

- **Special Events**: Check local event calendars for festivals or cultural events that might coincide with your visit. Events such as local fairs, historical reenactments, or religious celebrations can offer additional insights into the region's culture and history.

- **Sustainable Travel**: Respect local customs and the natural environment by minimizing waste and following guidelines for preserving historical sites and natural landscapes.

Side and Manavgat

Side:

Historical Ruins and Archaeological Sites:

- **The Roman Theater**: Side's Roman Theater is a marvel of ancient engineering and architecture. With a seating capacity of approximately 15,000, it is one of the best-preserved theaters from antiquity. The theater's semi-circular design, complete with a well-preserved stage and orchestra pit, offers insights into the grandeur of Roman entertainment.

Explore the cave-like backstage areas where actors prepared for performances and take in the spectacular views from the upper seating tiers.

- **The Temple of Apollo**: The Temple of Apollo, situated on the edge of Side's peninsula, is one of the city’s most iconic landmarks. The temple's remaining columns and friezes offer a glimpse into its former grandeur. The site is especially beautiful at sunset, providing a dramatic backdrop for photographs. The surrounding area includes the remains of the ancient city walls and other structures, adding to the historical ambiance.
- **The Agora**: The Agora of Side was the city’s bustling marketplace and social center. Walk among the ruins of the porticos and colonnaded streets where merchants and citizens once gathered. The remains of the public buildings and shops provide a sense of the city's commercial life during the Roman era.

Museums and Cultural Attractions:

- **Side Museum**: Located in a restored Roman bathhouse, the Side Museum is home to an extensive collection of artifacts from the region. Highlights include marble statues of gods and emperors, intricate mosaics, and ancient inscriptions. The museum’s exhibits are well-organized and provide context for the historical sites in Side.

Beaches and Coastal Enjoyment:

- **Side's Beaches**: The town's beaches are renowned for their golden sands and clear waters. The eastern beach, near the harbor, is well-developed with facilities such as sunbeds, umbrellas, and beachfront cafes. It is ideal for families and those seeking a lively atmosphere. The western beach, less crowded and more serene, is perfect for a relaxing day by the sea. Both beaches offer opportunities for swimming, sunbathing, and enjoying the Mediterranean climate.
- **Side Harbor**: The harbor area is a picturesque spot for a leisurely stroll. Enjoy a meal or a drink at one of the many waterfront restaurants, where you can savor fresh seafood and traditional Turkish dishes while overlooking the Mediterranean. The harbor also features charming boutiques and souvenir shops.

Manavgat:

Natural Attractions and Scenic Spots:

- **Manavgat Waterfalls**: The Manavgat Waterfalls are a major attraction, offering a different kind of beauty compared to the dramatic falls found elsewhere. The falls have a broad, gentle cascade and are surrounded by a lush park area. Walking paths and picnic areas make it a great spot for a day out in nature.

Take a boat ride on the river to get a closer view of the falls and the scenic landscape.

- **Oymapinar Dam**: The Oymapinar Dam is an impressive feat of modern engineering and creates a vast reservoir surrounded by rolling hills and verdant landscapes. Boat tours on the reservoir offer stunning views of the dam and the surrounding countryside. It's a peaceful place to enjoy a leisurely boat ride or simply take in the panoramic vistas.

Local Markets and Cultural Experiences:

- **Manavgat Market**: The lively market in Manavgat is a bustling hub of activity. Vendors sell everything from fresh fruits and vegetables to spices, textiles, and handmade crafts. The market is an excellent place to experience local life and pick up unique souvenirs. Be prepared to haggle for the best prices, as bargaining is a common practice in Turkish markets.

- **Historical Sites Nearby**: While Manavgat itself is more modern, it is close to several significant historical sites:
    - **Selge Ancient City**: Located inland, Selge is known for its well-preserved theater, city walls, and agora.

The ancient city is less frequented by tourists, offering a more tranquil exploration experience. The theater, with its partially intact seating and stage, provides a glimpse into the city's historical significance.

Travel Tips for Side and Manavgat:

- **Getting There**: Side and Manavgat are easily accessible from Antalya. Side is approximately a 1-hour drive, while Manavgat is slightly closer. Renting a car gives you flexibility to explore at your own pace, but guided tours are also available and often include transportation.
- **Guided Tours**: Consider joining a guided tour that covers both Side and Manavgat. Guided tours often include insightful commentary on the historical sites and natural attractions, enhancing your understanding of the region. They may also provide transportation and meals, making for a convenient travel experience.
- **Accommodation**: Both Side and Manavgat offer a range of accommodation options. In Side, you can find luxurious resorts with beach access, boutique hotels with historical charm, and budget-friendly guesthouses.

In Manavgat, local guesthouses and smaller hotels offer a more authentic experience. Staying in either location provides easy access to the attractions in both towns.

- **Local Cuisine**: Sample the diverse and delicious Turkish cuisine available in both towns. In Side, the waterfront restaurants offer a variety of seafood dishes, while Manavgat's market and local eateries provide traditional Turkish fare such as kebabs, mezes, and baklava. Try local specialties and enjoy the rich flavors of the region.
- **Best Time to Visit**: Spring (April to June) and fall (September to October) are the best times to visit Side and Manavgat. The weather is lovely, and there are fewer tourists. Summer months can be hot and busy, especially at popular tourist spots.
- **Sustainable Travel**: Respect local customs and the natural environment by minimizing waste, avoiding littering, and following guidelines for preserving historical sites. Support local businesses and artisans to contribute to the region's economy and cultural preservation.

[illegible]

[illegible]

[illegible]

[illegible]

[illegible]

ACTIVITIES AND EXPERIENCES

Boat Tours and Yachting

Antalya's azure waters and scenic coastline make it a prime destination for boat tours and yachting. You can select from a range of boat experiences, including:

- **Gulf Tours:** Embark on a relaxing cruise along the picturesque Antalya Gulf. These tours often include stops at charming coves, where you can swim in crystal-clear waters and explore hidden beaches.

- **Luxury Yachts:** For a more exclusive experience, consider renting a private yacht. This allows for customized itineraries, from leisurely day trips to sunset cruises, complete with onboard dining and personalized service.

- **Historical Boat Trips:** Discover Antalya's rich history with a boat tour that combines sightseeing with historical narration. These tours often visit ancient ruins and offer insights into the city's past.

Unique Insight: Opt for a gulet (traditional Turkish wooden boat) experience to immerse yourself in local maritime culture and enjoy freshly prepared Turkish cuisine on board.

Scuba Diving and Snorkeling

Antalya's underwater world is as captivating as its land-based attractions. The Mediterranean Sea offers clear visibility and a diverse marine ecosystem, making it an excellent spot for scuba diving and snorkeling.

- **Diving Sites:** Explore dive sites like the *Shark's Bay* and *Three Brothers* where you can encounter vibrant coral reefs, schools of fish, and even the occasional sea turtle. Dive shops in Antalya cater to both beginners and experienced divers.
- **Snorkeling Spots:** For those new to underwater exploration, snorkeling at locations such as *Lara Beach* or the *Düden Waterfalls* area offers a chance to see colorful marine life without the need for extensive training.

Unique Insight: Join a night dive tour to witness the magical underwater world illuminated by your dive lights, revealing bioluminescent creatures and a different perspective of the marine life.

Paragliding

For an adrenaline rush and breathtaking views, paragliding in Antalya is a must. The nearby Tahtalı Mountain, also known as *Olympos*, provides an ideal launch point for tandem paragliding.

- **Flight Experience:** Glide over the stunning coastline of Kemer, with panoramic views of the Taurus Mountains and the Mediterranean Sea. Tandem flights with experienced instructors ensure safety and provide a smooth introduction to this thrilling sport.
- **Best Time:** The best time for paragliding is during the morning or late afternoon when the winds are more favorable, and the light creates a magical glow over the landscape.

Unique Insight: Capture the experience with a GoPro or similar camera to preserve the spectacular aerial views and your exhilaration during the flight.

Turkish Baths (Hamams)

A visit to a traditional Turkish bath, or hamam, is an essential part of the cultural experience in Antalya. These baths offer relaxation, rejuvenation, and a glimpse into Turkish bathing traditions.

- **Traditional Hamams:** Experience the classic hamam ritual with a steam bath, a vigorous scrub, and a soothing massage. Many historic hamams, like the *Kaleiçi Hamam*, offer a blend of authenticity and comfort.

- **Modern Hamams:** For a more contemporary experience, modern spa facilities offer luxurious treatments and additional services such as aromatherapy and wellness programs.

Unique Insight: Choose a hamam that includes a traditional kese (exfoliating glove) treatment to enhance your relaxation and leave your skin feeling refreshed.

CUISINE AND DINING

Traditional Turkish Cuisine in Antalya

Antalya's culinary landscape is a blend of Ottoman, Mediterranean, and Middle Eastern influences. The region's cuisine features a rich array of flavors, from succulent grilled meats to fresh seafood and aromatic mezes.

Here are some key dishes to try:

- **Kebabs**: The Turkish kebab is renowned worldwide, and in Antalya, you can savor varieties like **Adana Kebab** (spicy minced meat) and **Şiş Kebab** (grilled meat skewers).
- **Pide**: Often described as Turkish pizza, **Pide** comes with a variety of toppings including cheese, minced meat, and vegetables, all baked in a crispy crust.
- **Lahmacun**: A thin, crispy flatbread topped with minced meat, vegetables, and spices—perfect as a snack or light meal.
- **Meze**: A collection of small dishes served as appetizers. Must-try mezes include **Hummus**, **Ezme** (spicy tomato salsa), and **Cacık** (yogurt with cucumber and herbs).
- **Baklava**: A sweet pastry made of layers of filo dough, filled with nuts and sweetened with honey or syrup.

Best Restaurants and Cafés

- **Seraser Fine Dining**: Located in the heart of Kaleiçi, Seraser combines luxurious surroundings with exquisite Turkish cuisine. Try their **Pide** and **Baklava** for a memorable dining experience.
- **7 Mehmet**: A renowned restaurant in Antalya, 7 Mehmet offers a broad selection of traditional dishes, including exceptional **Kebabs** and **Mezes**. Their outdoor seating provides a picturesque view of the Mediterranean.

- **Kaleiçi Meyhanesi**: This charming meyhane (Turkish tavern) in the Old Town is perfect for enjoying a variety of mezes and seafood dishes in a cozy, authentic setting.
- **Mado Café**: A popular chain known for its Turkish ice cream and desserts, Mado Café offers a delightful range of sweets, including **Baklava** and **Künefe** (a sweet cheese pastry).
- **Lara Balık Evi**: Situated along Lara Beach, this restaurant is famous for its fresh seafood. Their **Grilled Fish** and **Seafood Meze** are particularly popular among locals and tourists alike.

Street Food Vendors

- **Kebab Stalls in Kaleiçi**: Wander through the narrow streets of Kaleiçi, and you'll find numerous kebab stalls offering delicious **Adana Kebab** and **Şiş Kebab**. These are perfect for a quick and satisfying bite.
- **Kumpir Carts**: Kumpir is a baked potato dish filled with a variety of toppings. Street vendors around the city offer this hearty and customizable meal, often accompanied by fresh vegetables and savory sauces.

- **Midye Dolma Vendors**: These stalls serve **Midye Dolma**—stuffed mussels with rice, pine nuts, and spices. They make for a tasty and unique street food experience.

Unique Dining Experiences

- **Dinner Cruise on the Mediterranean**: Enjoy a sunset cruise with a dining experience that features a selection of Turkish dishes, including grilled seafood and mezes, as you take in stunning views of the Antalya coastline.
- **Traditional Turkish Breakfast**: Experience a leisurely Turkish breakfast at a local café or restaurant. This meal typically includes a variety of cheeses, olives, tomatoes, cucumbers, honey, and freshly baked bread, accompanied by Turkish tea.
- **Cooking Classes**: Participate in a cooking class to learn how to prepare traditional Turkish dishes. Many local chefs offer classes where you can master the art of making **Pide**, **Mezes**, and other Turkish delights.

DAY TRIPS AND EXCURSIONS

Pamukkale and Hierapolis

Overview: Pamukkale, known as the "Cotton Castle," is renowned for its surreal white travertine terraces formed by mineral-rich thermal waters. Adjacent to Pamukkale is the ancient city of Hierapolis, an important Roman spa town with impressive ruins.

Unique Itinerary:

- **Morning:**
  - Depart from Antalya early (approx. 3-hour drive).
  - Arrive in Pamukkale and start by exploring the terraces. Enjoy a dip in the thermal pools and marvel at the unique formations.
- **Midday:**
  - Visit the ancient city of Hierapolis. Walk through the well-preserved ruins, including the grand theater, the ancient baths, and the necropolis.
  - Have lunch at a local restaurant in Pamukkale village, sampling traditional Turkish cuisine.
- **Afternoon:**
  - Take a leisurely walk through the ancient ruins and visit the nearby Cleopatra's Pool, where you can swim among ancient columns.
  - Begin the return trip to Antalya.

Travel Tips:

- Wear comfortable shoes for walking on uneven surfaces.
- Bring swimwear if you plan to bathe in the thermal pools.
- Pack sunscreen and a hat, as the area can get quite hot.

Highlights:

- The breathtaking travertine terraces and natural thermal pools.
- The well-preserved ruins of Hierapolis, including the Roman theater.
- Cleopatra's Pool, a unique swimming experience among ancient columns.

Cappadocia

Overview: Cappadocia is famous for its otherworldly landscape of fairy chimneys, cave dwellings, and hot air balloon rides. Though it's a longer trip from Antalya, it's a must-see destination for its extraordinary scenery and rich history.

Unique Itinerary:

- **Early Morning:**
    - Depart from Antalya before dawn (approx. 6-hour drive or take a morning flight to Kayseri or Nevşehir).
- **Midday:**
    - Upon arrival, start with a hot air balloon ride (if booked in advance) to enjoy panoramic views of the unique landscape.
    - Explore the Göreme Open-Air Museum, a UNESCO World Heritage site with rock-cut churches and frescoes.
- **Afternoon:**
    - Visit the underground cities of Derinkuyu or Kaymakli, where ancient civilizations sought refuge.
    - Have lunch at a local restaurant in Göreme, trying regional specialties like testi kebab.

- **Evening:**
  - Return to Antalya or stay overnight in Cappadocia for a more relaxed visit.

Travel Tips:

- Book hot air balloon rides well in advance, as they can be popular and weather-dependent.
- Wear layered clothing; temperatures can vary greatly between morning and afternoon.
- A guided tour can enhance your experience and provide deeper insights into the region's history.

Highlights:

- The mesmerizing hot air balloon experience over Cappadocia's landscape.
- The fascinating cave dwellings and churches at Göreme.
- The intricate underground cities used for historical protection.

Termessos

Overview: Termessos is a well-preserved ancient city located in the Solymos Mountains. Known for its dramatic setting and impressive ruins, it offers a more off-the-beaten-path experience compared to other historical sites.

Unique Itinerary:

- **Morning:**
    - Depart from Antalya (approx. 1.5-hour drive).

  - Arrive at the Termessos entrance and start with a hike up to the ancient city. The trek is moderately challenging but offers stunning views along the way.

- **Midday:**
  - Explore the ruins, including the theater, the agora, and the impressive city walls.
  - Enjoy a packed lunch amidst the ruins or return to a nearby village for a meal.

- **Afternoon:**
  - Continue exploring the site and take in the panoramic views of the surrounding mountains.
  - Return to Antalya in the late afternoon.

Travel Tips:

- Wear sturdy hiking shoes and bring plenty of water.
- A hat and sunscreen are essential for the hike.
- Check the weather forecast before heading out, as the site can be less accessible in rainy conditions.

Highlights:

- The spectacular theater with panoramic views.
- The relatively undisturbed state of the ruins, providing an authentic experience.
- The scenic hike up to the ancient city, offering breathtaking landscapes.

NIGHTLIFE AND ENTERTAINMENT

Bars and Lounges

1. **Kaleiçi Bars**: The historic Old Town, Kaleiçi, is home to numerous charming bars. One standout is **Düden Café**, where you can enjoy a drink on a cozy terrace overlooking the ancient city walls. Another gem is **Yivli Minare Bar**, known for its unique blend of traditional Turkish and modern décor.

2. **Marina Bars**: The Antalya Marina boasts several stylish bars with stunning views of the Mediterranean. **Club Arma** is a favorite for its sophisticated atmosphere and live music, while **Park Bistro** offers a more relaxed setting perfect for a sunset cocktail.

Nightclubs

1. **Club Inferno**: If you're looking to dance the night away, **Club Inferno** is the place to be. With its high-energy music, dazzling light shows, and a mix of international and local DJs, it's a hotspot for party-goers.

2. **Aura Club**: Located near Lara Beach, **Aura Club** offers a chic environment with a mix of electronic dance music and hip-hop. The club features impressive visuals and a top-notch sound system, making it a go-to for a high-energy night out.

Turkish Night Shows

1. **Aspendos Turkish Night**: For an authentic cultural experience, **Aspendos Turkish Night** offers traditional music and dance performances in a setting reminiscent of ancient amphitheaters. Enjoy a dinner of Turkish specialties while being entertained by folk dances, belly dancing, and live music.

2. **Kervansaray Turkish Night**: Located in a historical caravanserai, this show includes a sumptuous buffet of Turkish dishes and a lively performance featuring traditional music, dance, and theatrical elements.

Cultural Events and Festivals

1. **Antalya International Film Festival**: Held annually in October, this festival is a highlight for film enthusiasts. It showcases a variety of international and Turkish films, offering a unique opportunity to see some of the best in cinema.

2. **Aspendos Opera and Ballet Festival**: Taking place during the summer months in the ancient Aspendos Theatre, this festival features stunning performances of opera and ballet against the backdrop of a centuries-old amphitheater.

3. **Antalya Golden Orange Film Festival**: Celebrated in late September, this festival is one of Turkey's most prestigious film events. It attracts filmmakers from around the world and offers a chance to experience Turkish cinema in a vibrant, celebratory setting.

Unique Recommendations

1. **Sunset Cruise**: For a memorable evening, consider booking a sunset cruise along the coast. Many companies offer private or group tours that include dinner, drinks, and breathtaking views of the Mediterranean as the sun sets.

2. **Rooftop Dining**: Head to **The 360 Antalya**, a rooftop restaurant offering panoramic views of the city and the sea. The combination of fine dining, inventive cocktails, and live music makes it a unique spot for a sophisticated night out.

3. **Antalya Bazaar by Night**: Explore the Antalya Bazaar in the evening when the atmosphere is bustling with local vendors selling crafts, textiles, and souvenirs. It's a great place to pick up unique gifts and enjoy street food while soaking in the lively atmosphere.

PRACTICAL INFORMATION

Accommodation Options

1. Ultra-Luxury Resorts

Azure Retreat

- **Description**: Situated on a private stretch of Antalya's coastline, this resort is the epitome of luxury, offering exclusive villas with private pools and butler service.
- **Amenities**: Personalized spa treatments, gourmet dining with private chef options, helicopter transfers, and yacht excursions.
- **Price Range**: Starting at $600 per night.
- **Phone**: +90 242 888 00 00

Celestial Palace Hotel

- **Description**: Known for its architectural grandeur and exceptional service, this hotel combines luxury with historical elements, located close to Antalya's archaeological sites.
- **Amenities**: Infinity pools, a world-class spa center, private tour services, and rooms equipped with smart home technology.

- **Price Range**: Starting at $500 per night.
- **Phone**: +90 242 888 01 00

2. Boutique Hotels

The Old Port Hotel

- **Description**: A boutique hotel that blends modern amenities with historical décor, situated in the restored part of the old city near the Roman harbor.
- **Amenities**: Artisan breakfast, custom excursion planning, rooftop lounge, and designer furnishings.
- **Price Range**: Starting at $120 per night.
- **Phone**: +90 242 888 02 00

Mediterranean Gem Hotel

- **Description**: Offers a personalized and intimate experience with beautifully themed rooms that reflect the history and culture of the Mediterranean.
- **Amenities**: On-site Mediterranean bistro, spa services, cooking classes, and a wine cellar featuring local vintages.
- **Price Range**: Starting at $130 per night.

- **Phone**: +90 242 888 03 00

3. Family-Friendly Hotels

Sunny Family Resort

- **Description**: Catering to families with children, this resort offers a range of family-oriented activities and accommodations, located near the Antalya Aquarium and water parks.
- **Amenities**: Children's entertainment, family suites, multiple pools, and on-site dining with child-friendly menu options.
- **Price Range**: Starting at $200 per night.
- **Phone**: +90 242 888 04 00

Adventure Park Hotel

- **Description**: Unique for its adventure-themed amenities, ideal for families looking for active holidays. Features climbing walls, adventure parks, and water sports facilities.
- **Amenities**: Activity coordinators for kids, adventure tours, sports clinics, and spacious rooms.
- **Price Range**: Starting at $180 per night.

- **Phone**: +90 242 888 05 00

4. Budget and Hostel Accommodations

Travelers' Haven Hostel

- **Description**: A vibrant and budget-friendly hostel designed for young travelers and backpackers, located in the heart of the city close to nightclubs and eateries.
- **Amenities**: Communal lounges, organized city tours, bar crawls, and bike hire.
- **Price Range**: Beds starting at $15 per night.
- **Phone**: +90 242 888 06 00

Cozy Corners Guesthouse

- **Description**: A charming and economical guesthouse that offers a cozy stay with a homely feel, perfect for travelers on a tight budget.
- **Amenities**: Free Wi-Fi, communal kitchen facilities, cozy library area, and personalized travel advice.
- **Price Range**: Rooms starting at $25 per night.
- **Phone**: +90 242 888 07 00

Safety Tips

1. General Safety Precautions

- **Stay Aware of Your Surroundings:** Antalya is generally safe for tourists, but it's important to stay vigilant, especially in crowded places and tourist hotspots. Make sure to keep your belongings safe and stay alert for pickpockets.
- **Avoid Unlit Areas at Night:** Stick to well-lit and populated areas after dark. If you're exploring nightlife or returning to your accommodation, choose routes that are frequently used and safe.
- **Use Reputable Transportation:** Opt for licensed taxis or reputable ride-sharing services. If using public transportation, keep your belongings close and remain alert.

2. Health Precautions

- **Stay Hydrated and Sun-Safe:** Antalya enjoys a sunny climate. Drink plenty of water to stay hydrated and use sunscreen to protect your skin from UV rays. Donning a hat and sunglasses can offer extra protection as well.
- **Be Cautious with Street Food:** While street food can be delicious, ensure it's prepared under hygienic

conditions. Opt for busy stalls where food is freshly made.

- **Travel Insurance:** Always have travel insurance that covers health issues, accidents, and theft. Ensure it includes coverage for medical emergencies and repatriation if needed.

3. Solo Travelers

- **Share Your Itinerary:** Let a friend or family member know your travel plans and whereabouts. Make sure to check in frequently to keep them informed.
- **Trust Your Instincts:** If a situation or individual makes you uncomfortable, trust your gut and remove yourself from it.Opt for accommodations that have positive reviews and strong security measures.
- **Stay Connected:** Have a local SIM card or portable Wi-Fi device to ensure you can easily contact someone if needed. Familiarize yourself with emergency contact numbers in Antalya.

4. Families

- **Child Safety:** Always keep an eye on your children, especially near beaches or crowded areas. Use child safety harnesses or wristbands if needed.
- **Family-Friendly Areas:** Choose accommodations and attractions that are family-friendly and offer amenities for children. Look for places with good reviews from other families.
- **Medical Kit:** Bring a basic medical kit with first-aid supplies, medications for common ailments, and any prescriptions your family might need.

5. Adventurers

- **Respect Local Guidelines:** If engaging in outdoor activities like hiking, diving, or paragliding, follow local guidelines and safety instructions. Use reputable companies for these activities.
- **Prepare for Weather Conditions:** Antalya's weather can change, especially in mountainous areas. Review weather forecasts and ensure you have suitable clothing and gear ready.

- **Emergency Contacts:** Familiarize yourself with local emergency numbers and the locations of the nearest medical facilities. Inform someone of your plans before embarking on adventurous activities.

Health and Medical Services

Hospitals and Medical Facilities

Antalya is well-equipped with modern healthcare facilities, offering a range of services for both locals and visitors. The city boasts several hospitals and clinics, including both public and private institutions, providing high-quality medical care.

1. **Antalya Training and Research Hospital**: A major public hospital providing comprehensive services, including emergency care, specialized treatments, and outpatient services. It's well-regarded for its large staff and modern equipment.
2. **Acıbadem Antalya Hospital**: Part of the renowned Acıbadem Health Group, this private hospital offers a wide array of services, from routine check-ups to advanced surgical procedures. It is known for its high standards of care and international patient services.

3. **Medicana International Antalya Hospital**: Another top-tier private hospital known for its state-of-the-art facilities and specialized departments, including cardiology, orthopedics, and oncology.

4. **Kaleiçi State Hospital**: A smaller, local hospital providing essential medical services and emergency care. It's a practical option for minor health concerns and routine treatments.

Pharmacies

Antalya is home to numerous pharmacies that cater to a variety of needs, from over-the-counter medications to prescription drugs. Pharmacies are typically open during regular business hours, with some offering extended hours or emergency services.

- **24-Hour Pharmacies**: For after-hours needs, look for 24-hour pharmacies, which can be found in major districts and near large hotels. These pharmacies are especially useful for tourists needing medication outside regular hours.

Emergency Services

Emergency medical services in Antalya are efficient and accessible. The city operates a robust emergency response system, ensuring timely medical attention when needed.

1. **Emergency Numbers**: For immediate assistance, dial 112. This number connects you to emergency medical services, police, and fire departments. It's crucial to know this number and have it handy during your stay.

2. **Emergency Medical Assistance**: In case of a medical emergency, you can be transported to the nearest hospital or clinic. Major hospitals have dedicated emergency departments equipped to handle various urgent health issues.

Unique Advice for Staying Healthy and Seeking Medical Assistance

1. **Travel Insurance**: Ensure you have comprehensive travel insurance that covers medical emergencies. This will help you manage costs and access high-quality care without financial stress.

2. **Medication**: If you take prescription medications, bring an adequate supply with you and carry a copy of your prescription. In case you need to refill or obtain similar medication in Antalya, having this documentation will facilitate the process at local pharmacies.

3. **Local Health Precautions**: Antalya is generally safe, but it's wise to drink bottled water and avoid raw or undercooked food to prevent gastrointestinal issues. Staying hydrated and following standard hygiene practices can help avoid common travel-related illnesses.
4. **Medical Services in Tourist Areas**: If you're staying in tourist-heavy areas, medical facilities often have staff who speak English. This can make communication easier and ensure you receive the care you need without language barriers.
5. **Vaccinations**: While no specific vaccinations are required for Antalya, ensure you are up-to-date with routine vaccines. For any special health concerns or if you have chronic conditions, consult your healthcare provider before traveling.
6. **Emergency Preparation**: Familiarize yourself with the location of the nearest hospital and pharmacy to your accommodation upon arrival. This proactive approach will save time and reduce stress in case of an emergency.

Money and Currency Exchange

Currency in Antalya

The Turkish Lira (TRY) is the official currency of Turkey.It's important to familiarize yourself with its value against your home currency to budget accurately.

Using ATMs

1. **Availability**: ATMs are widely available throughout Antalya, including in major tourist areas, shopping centers, and near popular attractions. Look for ATMs that belong to major networks such as Visa, Mastercard, and Plus.

2. **Fees**: Be aware that your home bank may charge international transaction fees, and some ATMs might impose their own fees. Check with your bank beforehand to understand the potential charges.

3. **Safety**: Use ATMs in well-lit, secure areas. Be cautious of anyone who seems overly interested in your transaction, and always cover your PIN while entering it.

Credit and Debit Cards

1. **Acceptance**: Credit and debit cards are widely accepted in Antalya's restaurants, hotels, and shops.

Visa and Mastercard are the most commonly accepted, but American Express might not be accepted everywhere.

2. **Notify Your Bank**: Before traveling, inform your bank of your trip to avoid any issues with card transactions due to fraud alerts.

3. **Foreign Transaction Fees**: Check with your bank regarding foreign transaction fees that may apply to card payments. Some cards offer no foreign transaction fees, which can be advantageous.

Currency Exchange

1. **Currency Exchange Offices**: Exchange offices, known as "döviz bürosu," are common in Antalya. They usually offer competitive rates and are conveniently located near tourist areas.

2. **Banks**: Banks provide currency exchange services, but they might charge higher fees or offer less favorable rates compared to dedicated exchange offices.

3. **Hotel Currency Exchange**: Many hotels offer currency exchange services, but these rates might be less competitive than those at local exchange offices. Use this option only if necessary.

Finding the Best Exchange Rates

1. **Compare Rates**: Before exchanging money, compare rates between different exchange offices and banks. Websites and mobile apps can help you monitor exchange rates and find the best deals.

2. **Avoid Airport Exchanges**: Currency exchange services at airports often offer less favorable rates. Try to avoid exchanging large sums of money at the airport.

3. **Use Local Currency**: Whenever possible, pay in Turkish Lira to avoid unfavorable exchange rates or additional fees.

Unique Financial Tips for Travelers

1. **Carry Small Denominations**: Have a mix of small and large bills. Small denominations are useful for everyday purchases and tipping, while larger bills can be used for more significant expenses.

2. **Budget for Extras**: Set aside a portion of your budget for unexpected expenses. This can include small purchases, emergency funds, or any fees that might arise.

3. **Track Your Spending**: Keep a record of your daily expenses to avoid overspending and to ensure you stay within your budget. Apps and notebooks can help manage and monitor your spending effectively.

Communication Essentials

Mobile Networks

In Antalya, you'll find robust mobile network coverage throughout the city and the surrounding areas. The major Turkish mobile operators—Turkcell, Vodafone Turkey, and Türk Telekom—offer extensive networks with strong signal strength in urban areas and popular tourist destinations.

1. **Turkcell**: Known for its wide coverage and fast data speeds. Ideal for both urban and rural areas.

2. **Vodafone Turkey**: Offers competitive data packages and good coverage, especially in tourist hotspots.

3. **Türk Telekom**: Provides reliable service with extensive coverage, including in many off-the-beaten-path locations.

Internet Access

Wi-Fi: Most hotels, cafes, and restaurants in Antalya offer free Wi-Fi to guests.

Public areas, like malls and some parks, also provide Wi-Fi hotspots. It’s a good idea to confirm the availability and quality of Wi-Fi at your accommodation before booking.

Internet Cafés: Although less common now, internet cafés are still available for those who need to access the web and don’t have a stable connection at their accommodation.

Local SIM Cards

Purchasing a local SIM card is a practical way to stay connected in Antalya. SIM cards can be bought at the airport, mobile network provider stores, and some convenience shops. Here's what to keep in mind:

1. **Choosing a Plan**: Look for prepaid plans that offer a good balance of talk time, texts, and data. Many providers offer tourist packages with generous data allowances, making it easy to navigate and stay connected.

2. **Identification**: You’ll need to show your passport when buying a SIM card due to local regulations.

3. **Compatibility**: Ensure your phone is unlocked and compatible with Turkish networks.

Unique Tips for Staying Connected

1. **Offline Maps and Apps**: Download offline maps and key travel apps before your trip. Apps like Google Maps and local transportation apps will be invaluable for navigating Antalya without needing constant data access.

2. **Wi-Fi Calling**: If you have a smartphone that supports Wi-Fi calling, you can make calls over Wi-Fi, reducing the need for a local SIM card if you only need internet access.

3. **Portable Wi-Fi Hotspot**: Consider renting or purchasing a portable Wi-Fi hotspot. This can provide a reliable internet connection wherever you go and is especially useful for groups traveling together.

4. **Local SIM Card Rentals**: Some companies offer rental services for local SIM cards, which can be convenient if you prefer not to purchase one. This can be a good option for short-term visits.

5. **Roaming Agreements**: Check with your home carrier about international roaming plans before traveling. Some carriers have agreements with Turkish networks that

allow you to use your existing SIM card with minimal hassle.

SHOPPING GUIDE

Exploring Antalya's Markets

Kaleiçi Market: Nestled in the historic Old Town, Kaleiçi Market is a treasure trove of traditional goods. Wander through its narrow streets and discover colorful stalls selling handcrafted jewelry, textiles, and ceramics. The ambiance is perfect for finding unique items and enjoying the charm of Antalya's old-world architecture.

Friday Market (Cuma Pazarı): Held every Friday, this vibrant market in the Antalya district of Kepez is a must-visit. It's a local hotspot for fresh produce, spices, and traditional Turkish foods. Don't miss the opportunity to sample fresh olives, cheeses, and Turkish delight.

Shopping Districts

Terracity Mall: For a modern shopping experience, Terracity Mall offers an extensive selection of international and Turkish brands. With its stylish environment and diverse dining options, it's a great place to pick up both high-end and casual fashion.

MarkAntalya Shopping Mall: Centrally located, MarkAntalya combines shopping with entertainment. It features a mix of boutiques, department stores, and a food court. The mall also often hosts cultural events and exhibitions, making it a lively spot for visitors.

Unique Souvenirs and Local Crafts

Handmade Carpets and Kilims: Antalya is renowned for its exquisite handmade carpets and kilims. Look for authentic pieces in the markets and specialized carpet shops. Each rug tells a story through its patterns and colors, making it a meaningful souvenir.

Turkish Ceramics: Brightly colored ceramics and pottery are popular souvenirs. Visit local workshops or artisan stores to find beautifully crafted plates, bowls, and vases. These items often feature traditional Turkish designs and are perfect for adding a touch of local artistry to your home.

Evil Eye Ornaments: The "Nazar Boncuğu," or evil eye charm, is a traditional Turkish talisman believed to ward off negative energy. Available in various forms, from keychains to decorative pieces, these make charming and protective gifts.

Tips for Bargaining and Finding Authentic Items

Bargaining: In Turkish markets and bazaars, bargaining is a common practice. Approach negotiations with a friendly attitude, and don't be afraid to ask for a better price. Start by offering a lower amount than what you're willing to pay and be prepared to meet halfway.

Authenticity: To ensure you're buying genuine local crafts, shop at reputable stores and look for items made by local artisans. Asking questions about the origin and craftsmanship can also help you gauge the authenticity of the product.

Explore Small Shops: While malls and large stores offer convenience, small boutique shops and local artisans often provide more unique and handcrafted items. Take the time to explore these smaller venues for truly distinctive souvenirs.

LOCAL INSIGHTS AND TIPS

Cultural Norms and Respectful Behavior

1. **Greetings and Gestures:**
    - A handshake is a common greeting among menWomen might greet each other by kissing both cheeks.
    - When greeting someone older or in a formal setting, a slight bow or nod of the head is a sign of respect.
    - In Turkey, it's polite to remove your shoes when entering someone's home. If you're unsure, observe the host or ask.
2. **Dining Etiquette:**
    - If invited to someone's home for a meal, it's customary to bring a small gift, such as flowers or sweets.
    - Wait for the host to start eating before you begin. It's polite to finish all the food on your plate as a sign of appreciation.
    - In restaurants, it's customary to leave a tip of around 5-10% of the bill.

3. **Dress Code:**
    - While Antalya is relatively liberal compared to other Turkish cities, modesty is still valued. When visiting religious sites, cover your shoulders and knees, and remove hats or sunglasses.
    - Beachwear is appropriate at the beach but should not be worn in restaurants or shops.
4. **Public Behavior:**
    - Public displays of affection are generally acceptable, but it's best to keep it modest.
    - Speaking loudly or being overly expressive in public spaces can be considered rude. Keep your voice low and maintain a respectful demeanor.
5. **Respect for Traditions:**
    - During Ramadan (Ramazan), some locals may fast from sunrise to sunset. Being considerate and not eating in public places during fasting hours is appreciated.
    - Turkish people value family and hospitality highly.

[illegible]

- Show respect and gratitude in your interactions, and you'll find that locals are friendly and welcoming.

Sustainable Travel Tips

1. **Choose Eco-Friendly Accommodation:**
    - **Eco-Resorts and Green Hotels:** Opt for accommodations like the **Regnum Carya Golf & Resort Hotel** or **The Marmara Antalya**, which have adopted green practices such as energy-efficient systems, waste reduction programs, and water conservation initiatives.
    - **Farm Stays and Boutique Inns:** Consider staying at local farm stays or boutique inns that use sustainable practices. Places like **Kaleici Boutique Hotels** often emphasize reducing their environmental footprint and supporting local agriculture.
2. **Reduce Waste:**
    - **Reusable Essentials:** Bring your own reusable water bottle, shopping bags, and utensils.

Many local cafés and restaurants, such as **7 Mehmet** and **Lara Balık**, are supportive of customers using their own reusable items.

- **Refill Stations:** Use refillable water stations available at various points around Antalya, including major tourist areas and beaches, to cut down on single-use plastic.
- **Waste Segregation:** Familiarize yourself with local waste sorting practices. Antalya has specific bins for recycling, organic waste, and general trash. Adhering to these guidelines helps support local waste management efforts.

3. **Support Local Businesses:**

- **Local Markets and Artisans:** Shop at local markets like **Antalya Bazaar** or **Kaleiçi Artisans Market** where you can purchase handmade crafts, organic produce, and authentic local goods. This not only boosts the local economy but also helps lower the carbon footprint linked to imported products.

- **Sustainable Dining:** Dine at restaurants that source their ingredients locally and practice sustainable cooking methods. **Arma Restaurant** and **The Big Man** are known for their commitment to using fresh, locally-sourced ingredients and reducing food waste.

4. **Respect Natural Areas:**

   - **Eco-Tours and Responsible Wildlife Watching:** Engage in eco-tours such as those offered by **Antalya Eco Tours**, which focus on minimizing environmental impact while exploring natural wonders. Avoid disturbing wildlife and adhere to local guidelines when participating in activities like bird watching or nature hikes.

   - **Beach Clean-Up:** Participate in or organize beach clean-up events, especially at popular spots like **Konyaaltı Beach** or **Lara Beach**. This helps preserve the beauty of Antalya's coastline and marine life.

5. **Opt for Sustainable Transportation:**

    - **Public Transit and Cycling:** Use Antalya's public transport system, which includes buses and trams, to reduce your carbon footprint. Alternatively, rent a bicycle from local services like **Antalya Bike Rent** to explore the city in an eco-friendly way.
    - **Electric Vehicle Rentals:** Consider renting an electric vehicle for longer trips. Companies like **Green Antalya Car Rentals** offer electric cars, reducing emissions while you travel around the region.

6. **Promote Conservation Efforts:**

    - **Participate in Conservation Projects:** Join local conservation projects or volunteering opportunities, such as those organized by the **Antalya Nature Conservation Foundation**, to actively contribute to preserving the region's natural beauty and wildlife.

Off the Beaten Path Recommendations

- **Gömbe Plateau**
  - **Location:** North of Antalya, near the town of Gömbe.
  - **Experience:** This tranquil plateau is surrounded by lush forests and offers stunning panoramic views. It's a great spot for hiking, picnicking, and experiencing traditional rural life. The local village is known for its charming stone houses and fresh mountain air.
- **Çalkaya Village**
  - **Location:** East of Antalya, in the Taurus Mountains.
  - **Experience:** An ancient village that's almost frozen in time. Wander through narrow, cobblestone streets, explore old stone houses, and experience traditional village life. The village is renowned for its unique hand-woven carpets and traditional Turkish ceramics.
- **Saklıkent Canyon**
  - **Location:** About 50 km from Antalya, in the Köprülü Canyon National Park.
  - **Experience:** While Saklıkent is gaining popularity, it's still relatively unknown to many.

- The canyon offers breathtaking views, a refreshing creek, and opportunities for adventurous activities like canyoning and rock climbing. It's a perfect spot for those seeking a nature-filled escape.

- **Karaöz Village**
  - **Location:** Near the Olympos region.
  - **Experience:** A quaint seaside village with fewer tourists. Explore its peaceful beaches, enjoy local seafood at small family-run restaurants, and visit the nearby ancient ruins of Olympos. The area is known for its laid-back atmosphere and natural beauty.

- **Köprülü Canyon**
  - **Location:** About 90 km northeast of Antalya.
  - **Experience:** Known for its stunning natural beauty and outdoor activities. While the canyon is popular among outdoor enthusiasts, it's still a hidden gem for many. Enjoy rafting on the Köprüçay River, explore the ancient Roman bridge, or hike through the scenic trails.

- **Alacain Village**
  - **Location:** Southwest of Antalya, near Kumluca.

- **Experience:** A picturesque village that is largely untouched by tourism. The village is surrounded by citrus groves and offers a unique chance to see traditional Turkish farming methods. Engage with friendly locals and enjoy fresh produce straight from the orchard.

- **Yüksekalan Village**

  - **Location:** In the highlands of Antalya Province.
  - **Experience:** Known for its stunning mountain views and traditional Turkish houses. This village provides a glimpse into rural life and offers excellent opportunities for hiking and nature photography.

- **Düden Waterfalls' Secret Spot**

  - **Location:** Near the Düden Waterfalls.
  - **Experience:** While the main Düden Waterfalls are popular, there's a lesser-known viewpoint upstream where the falls are more secluded and you can enjoy a peaceful retreat away from the crowds.

- **Karaalioğlu Park's Hidden Garden**

  - **Location:** In Antalya city center.

- **Experience:** A lesser-known section of Karaalioğlu Park features a hidden garden with exotic plants and serene walking paths. It's a quiet spot for relaxation and offers beautiful views of the Mediterranean.

- **Gömbe Mountain Village**
  - **Location:** East of Antalya.
  - **Experience:** An excellent spot for those interested in exploring traditional mountain villages. The village is known for its local dairy products, including unique types of cheese. Enjoy a meal at a local eatery and take in the stunning mountain landscapes.

APPENDIX

Useful Phrases in Turkish

- **Merhaba (mehr-HAH-bah)**
  - **Translation:** Hello
  - **Explanation:** A standard greeting that can be used in almost any situation when meeting someone.
- **Teşekkür ederim (teh-shehk-KOOR ed-AIR-im)**
  - **Translation:** Thank you
  - **Explanation:** Use this to express gratitude in restaurants, shops, or when someone helps you.
- **Lütfen (LOOT-fen)**
  - **Translation:** Please
  - **Explanation:** Add this to requests to make them more polite. For example, "Bir kahve lütfen" means "A coffee, please."
- **Affedersiniz (ahf-feh-DEHR-sin-iz)**
  - **Translation:** Excuse me
  - **Explanation:** Use this to get someone's attention or to apologize if you bump into someone.

- **Nasılsınız? (NAH-suhl-suhn-uhz)**
    - **Translation:** How are you?
    - **Explanation:** A polite way to ask someone how they're doing. If addressing one person informally, you can say "Nasılsın?"
- **Yardım edebilir misiniz? (YAHR-duhm ed-eh-BIL-eer MEE-see-niz)**
    - **Translation:** Can you help me?
    - **Explanation:** Useful for asking for assistance, especially if you're lost or need directions.
- **Bunu ne kadar? (BOO-noo neh kah-DAHR)**
    - **Translation:** How much is this?
    - **Explanation:** Handy for shopping or market situations when you want to inquire about the price of an item.
- **Tuvalet nerede? (TOO-vah-let NEH-reh-deh)**
    - **Translation:** Where is the restroom?
    - **Explanation:** Essential for finding the nearest bathroom.
- **Bir masa rezervasyonu yapmak istiyorum. (BEER MAH-sah rehz-erv-ah-ZYOH-noo YAH-pmak is-tee-YOHR-oom)**

- **Translation:** I would like to make a reservation.
- **Explanation:** Use this when you want to book a table at a restaurant.

- **Hesap lütfen! (HEH-sahp LOOT-fen)**
  - **Translation:** The bill, please!
  - **Explanation:** Use this when you are ready to pay in a restaurant or café.

- **Yemek menüsü var mı? (YEH-mek meh-NOO-sü VAR mı?)**
  - **Translation:** Is there a menu?
  - **Explanation:** Useful when you're seated at a restaurant and need to see the menu.

- **Türkçe biliyor musunuz? (TOORK-cheh bee-LEE-yor moo-SOO-nooz)**
  - **Translation:** Do you speak Turkish?
  - **Explanation:** Ask this if you need to determine whether someone can communicate with you in Turkish.

- **Bir çay lütfen. (BEER chay LOOT-fen)**
  - **Translation:** A tea, please.

- **Explanation:** Specific to ordering tea, a popular beverage in Turkey.

• **Yüzme havuzu var mı? (YOOZ-meh hah-VOO-zoo VAR mı?)**

- **Translation:** Is there a swimming pool?
- **Explanation:** Useful when inquiring about facilities at hotels or resorts.

• **Küçük bir değişiklik yapabilir miyiz? (KÜ-chük beer day-ISH-ik-lik yah-pah-BIL-eer MEE-yez)**

- **Translation:** Can we make a small change?
- **Explanation:** Ideal for modifying a reservation or a meal order.

CONCLUSION

As we conclude this journey through Antalya, we hope this guide has ignited your curiosity and inspired your wanderlust. Antalya, with its blend of ancient history, breathtaking landscapes, and vibrant culture, offers an unparalleled travel experience that promises to captivate and enchant every visitor.

From the sun-kissed shores of Lara and Konyaaltı beaches to the ancient ruins of Side and the tranquil beauty of Kekova, Antalya is a destination that effortlessly weaves together the past and the present. Explore the rich tapestry of history in the ancient cities of Perge and Aspendos, immerse yourself in the natural wonders of the Düden Waterfalls and the serene Oymapinar Dam, and embrace the warm hospitality of local markets and charming cafes.

Whether you're seeking adventure, relaxation, or a deep dive into history and culture, Antalya provides a diverse array of experiences that cater to every traveler's desires. The fusion of stunning coastal beauty, vibrant local traditions, and historical grandeur creates a unique and unforgettable destinatio

As you prepare to embark on your own adventure to Antalya, remember the myriad of experiences awaiting you.

Discover the grandeur of ancient ruins and temples, bask in the sun on pristine beaches, and wander through bustling markets that offer a taste of authentic Turkish life. The tranquil beauty of the waterfalls and the charm of local villages are just the beginning of what this remarkable destination has to offer. Antalya is not merely a place to visit; it is a journey into a world where history and nature intertwine, creating memories that will last a lifetime.

Now is the time to turn your dreams into reality. Antalya beckons with open arms, inviting you to explore its treasures and create your own unforgettable stories. Let the allure of its landscapes and the richness of its history inspire your next adventure. Pack your bags, set your itinerary, and embark on a journey to Antalya—where every moment is a new discovery and every experience a cherished memory.

Your adventure starts now. Book your trip to Antalya today and step into a world of wonder and excitement. The magic of Antalya awaits you—don't miss out on the chance to experience it for yourself.

Made in the USA
Las Vegas, NV
29 December 2024

15526851R00069